The
Power of Purpose

By
WILLIAM GEORGE JORDAN
Author of "Kingship of Self-Control," "Majesty of Calmness," "Crown of Individuality"

William George Jordan

William George Jordan was born on 6 March 1864 in New York City, USA. He took his university education at the *City College of New York* and began his literary career as an editor of *Book Chat* in 1884. After a brief spell (1888-91) editing *Current Literature* - a magazine offering an eclectic combination of literature review and contemporary commentary, Jordan relocated to Chicago. It was here that he first lectured on his system of Mental Training; although not with any great success. In 1897 Jordan moved back to New York and was hired as the managing editor for *The Ladies Home Journal,* after which he moved on to edit *The Saturday Evening Post.* This substantial editing career is not Jordan's best known achievement however – his essays and thoughts on education and 'mental training' have garnered the most attention. In July 1891 *The Chicago Inter-Ocean* printed an interview with Jordan on his 'mental training'. After the article was published he received so many inquiries that he scheduled a long lecture tour on the subject. *The Inter-Ocean* reported that 'during the past few weeks the calls from Chicago have been so numerous, enthusiastic and positive for lecture courses and private society classes that he has concluded to resign his position in New York and come to Chicago.' In 1894, Jordan published a short pamphlet; *Mental Training, A Remedy for Education,* which opened with the following lines; 'here are two great things that education should do for the individual—it should train his senses, and teach him to think. Education, as we know it to-day, does not truly do either; it gives the individual only a vast accumulation of facts, unclassified, undigested, and seen in no true relations. Like seeds kept in a box, they may be retained, but they do not grow.' Jordan's allegorical style was widely utilised in all his works, and he penned his first book, *The Kingship of Self-Control,* in 1898. This was followed by a further nine texts, all on the subject of self-improvement; a theme which he continued writing on for the rest of his life. *The Majesty of Calmness* (1900) was perhaps his most popular self-help book. Despite these successes, Jordan's most influential writing was actually a political tract. In *The House of Governors* (1907), he aimed to 'promote uniform legislation on vital questions, to conserve states' rights, to lessen centralisation, to secure a fuller, freer voice of the people and to make a stronger nation.' The work was circulated to each state governor and to President Theodore Roosevelt, and was incredibly well received. His ideas were put into practice and the first 'meeting of the governors' was held in Washington, on 18 January, 1910 – with Jordan as its secretary. He was dropped as secretary a year later, but nevertheless, this group is a key part of his legacy.

At the age of fifty-eight, Jordan married Nellie Blanche Mitchell, in New York City at the Grace Episcopal Church. The marriage was a happy one, for the short time it lasted, but sadly Jordan died just six years later of pneumonia on 20 April 1928, at his home in New York.

Contents

CHAP.   PAGE

I.   POWER OF INDIVIDUAL PURPOSE   .   7

II.   THE INSPIRATION OF POSSIBILITIES .   14

III.   FACING THE MISTAKES OF LIFE   .   21

IV.   WHEN WE FORGET THE EQUITY   .   30

V.   THE CROWN OF INDIVIDUALITY   .   39

VI.   THE OPTIMISM THAT REALLY COUNTS   49

VII.   THE DARK VALLEY OF PROSPERITY   .   57

I

Power of Individual Purpose

PURPOSE gives a new impulse, a new impetus, a new interpretation to living. Purpose is the backbone of a life of courage. It shows that the highest justification for living is love—in some form. It may be for a cause, a country, an ideal, a family, or an individual. Purpose at its best means our kingship over conditions, our mastery over self, our dedication to something higher than self, fighting for the right and fighting it to the end. Were we able to follow even a great purpose from its highest flights of effort we might find its nest of inspiration—in the heart of some one of whom the world knew nothing.

Purpose makes man his own second creator and by it he can make himself largely what he will. He can choose his own realm: he can live contentedly in the mud of low desires like a lizard or sweep boldly high in the pure, inspiring, bracing air of noble ideals like an eagle rightfully claiming the mountain tops as its own.

If our aim be low, mean and selfish, bringing out all that is weakness in our nature, an ambition that betrays its method in the despicable things employed to attain it, it is unworthy of our crown of individuality.

Low purpose makes us experts in petty sophistries; it kills natural sweetness and kindness; it raises the moral temperature to a fever heat of "don't care" and lowers the vitality of all our higher living. This is not the purpose of which we speak; it is individuality at a discount, not at a premium—as we should hold it.

Purpose makes man a crusader—for something. He seems to grow greater before our eyes in his efforts to reach and grasp the cross of some ideal—though it may seem to us unattainable—when the inspiration and glow of the struggle itself means more to him than even a crown of victory. Purpose is conscious, continuous concentration to attain an end. Before it can be greatest there must be union and unity—body, mind, heart and soul acting together, as the essence of many flowers may be fused into a single perfume.

To many of us the eagles of purpose of the world's exalted great ones may be impossible to us in our present conditions. We may be bound by duties, cares, burdens, the daily problem of mere living that make great deeds difficult. But we can all have purpose and should have it and we should live to it at its best. We must finally be judged not by attainments but by the ideals and motives that inspired them. There is one purpose that no one is too humble to live by. It is— "faithfulness in little things." It may be only a new impetus of loyalty, trustfulness and watchfulness in our daily duties.

Employers find great difficulty in getting this very faithfulness in little things. Many of those paid for service are only eye-servants. They are listless, lazy, and irritably languid except—when off duty. They regard the repeated instructions as to how certain simple work should be done with an airy nonchalance that is indifferent, impudent and impertinent. They forget everything except some trifle of personal interest ; this is tattooed into their memory. They collapse under the slightest strain of responsibility like an intoxicated man leaning against an imaginary post. They are a bundle of excuses—where their own failures, foibles or flaws are under discussion.

Workers such as these consider merely getting a maximum pay-envelope at a minimum expense of mental or physical energy.

They wonder why some other worker is retained or promoted while they are sure they have worked just as long as she has each day. They forget they have not worked as wide or as deep—they overlook these two other dimensions. It is the *plus* of purpose consecrated to doing daily one's best with a constantly added increase of ability that makes the real difference. This simple phase of purpose may change the life of an individual and inspire ever higher purpose.

The conquest of a weakness in character, the acquirement of a new language, a concentrated attempt to be of greater usefulness to others in some way, to prove equal to our possibilities as they progressively grow larger under attainment—these may be, but purpose in a small way. Purpose unites the separate days of our living by the thread of continuity—as scattered beads form a necklace by the golden strand running through them. A mother may make even the care of her home and her family a *real* purpose if she puts into her labours the best that is in her, ever realizing she has her crown of individuality she must never forget.

Many men in this life, men of position, power, wealth and opportunity, are—merely drifting. They are not victors of their course but victims of the current. They live but have no definite purpose in living. In easy-going, careless, free way they are carried along by the tides of life, with no self-consciousness that they are drifters. Some of them do no defined great evil but no real good. If they were to do some great evil or fall before some great sorrow or trial it might be the means of startling them into realization, shocking them into vivid consciousness of their lack of purpose. Man does not drift into goodness,—the chance port of an aimless voyage. He must fight ever for his destination, ready to battle, with calmness and constant courage, against fog, darkness, adverse winds, and dangers that should only inspire to greater effort.

There is hardly any peril of the sea more dreaded by mariners than—a derelict. It carries no lights on bow or stern, no passengers, no rudder, no pilot, no crew. It is bound nowhere, carrying no cargo, to no port. Helpless in itself it is a menace to all others. Human derelicts are those ignored as hopeless by others, but they were first deserted by themselves. Lack of definite real purpose is the royal road to drifting, desertion, and derelict.

In seeking material success it may be

necessary to grasp a low rung of the ladder; but on the ladder of purpose begin with the highest rung your outstretched hand can clasp and hold on till you reach the next. Purpose takes man out of the orchestra of life and puts him on the stage of real action. It makes him part of the spectacle, not a mere spectator. It gives him a real part to play, one no other could play, in the great drama of humanity.

The great thing in life is not in realizing a purpose, but in fighting for it. If we feel the possibilities of a great work looming large before us and impelling us to action it is our duty to consecrate ourselves to it. Failure in a great work is nobler than success in a petty one that is beneath our maximum of possibility. We have nothing to do with results—they do not belong to us, anyway. It is our duty to do our best bravely and then to rest in the comfort of this fact alone. But be our work great or small let us have real purpose in life and battle for it undaunted to the end.

Purpose at its best must be above and be-yond us like the polar star that guides and in-spires the compass of the mariner. The world needs, more than talent, genius, wealth, or power, men of simple, earnest purpose, men consecrated to daily living in the inspiring illumination of an ideal ; men who make each day count directly for something real, who face each day's sunset with new harvests of good for those around them and for the world.

Being good, merely good in a pale, anemic, temperamental way is not enough. If the world is not daily better because we have lived, if the little circle of those around is not brightened, strengthened, heartened, helped, and some way made happier by our direct effort in our conscious living, we are not true to purpose or possibilities.   We cannot all be Lincolns and save a nation, but we can put the spirit of Lincoln into every trifle of our living—his simplicity, courage, kindness, love, consecration, justice.   The greatest good to the world is not the magnificent power of a few great men manifesting it on a colossal scale, but these same qualities, in a smaller, humbler way, manifested in millions of simple, unknown lives throughout the world.

II

The Inspiration of Possibilities

THE world needs the clarion call of a great inspiration on the unmeasured possibilities of the individual. No man that ever lived exhausted his possibilities. The greatest that ever shed the glory of their presence on this earth of ours have given but at most a few-sided showing of the lines upon which they concentrated. None ever lived the full, rounded, perfect flowering of his whole nature—the vastness of his possibility remained in the silence and secrecy of the unexpressed. Life is too short for the full story. The feeling of the incompleteness of this life, its unsatisfiedness, is a strong base of belief in—immortality.

Let us throw overboard that benumbing philosophy of the words "Remember your limitations" and preach ever : "Remember your limitless possibilities." With the new dignity added to the individual life comes a finer realization of the power of maximum living from day to day, a large, firmer grip on individual problems. There will be a revelation that must tend to kill shams and pretense. There will be a truer attunement with the highest real things in life. There will not be the folly—the disheartening "limitation" adage so fears—of people attempting to succeed at once in lines where only genius or years of consecrated effort can hope to achieve.

Man is not put into the world as a music-box mechanically set with a certain fixed number of tunes, but as a violin with infinite possibilities. This music no one can bring forth but the individual himself. He is placed into life not a finality, but a beginning; not a manufactured article, but raw material; not a statue, but an unhewn stone ready alike for the firm chisel of defined purpose or the subtle attrition of circumstances and conditions.

It is only what a man makes of himself that really counts. He must disinfect his mind from that weakening thought that he has an absolutely predetermined capacity like a freight-car with its weight and tonnage painted on the side. He is growing, expansive, unlimited, self-adjusting to increased responsibility, progressively able for large duties and higher possibilities as he realizes them and lives up to them.

Man should feel this sense of the limitless —physically, mentally, morally, spiritually. Newspaper and magazine stories of men who came to this country with seventy-six cents and now own thirty million dollars and head a trust tell the financial side of possibility. It is here deemed unnecessary to give *new* appetizers for a national hunger—so well developed.

From the physical side man may realize as a removed " limitation " that some of the strongest, most healthy and athletic men were weaklings in childhood and even young manhood. They made themselves anew by exercise, outdoor life, sunshine, simple food and adherence to the laws of health which constitute the common sense of Nature. There is no loss of any of the senses nor of limbs that has proved a handicap fatal to success of those great ones who had culti- vated a fine contempt for obstacles that dared to daunt them.

The possibilities of mental development stand vindicated in the splendid roster of the great ones of the world who, with smallest opportunities of education, fought their way to the ranks of great thinkers, men of rare individuality, and real leaders in the world's advance guard to the higher things.   Never were books so cheap or so accessible as to-day and but a trifle of time consecrated daily to this development would work wonders for him who not merely wishes and wants but *wills* to realize possibilities.

No one in life occupies a position so humble, be it in the smallest hamlet or the largest city, that he cannot manifest his moral strength and exercise it. There is none so obscure that he cannot make the lives of those around him marvellously changed, brightened and inspired if he would merely progressively live up to his expanding possibilities in the way of kindness, thoughtfulness, cheer, good-will, influence and optimism.

Better far is it for the individual to be a live coal, radiating light and heat for a day, than to be an icicle for a century. It is better to be an oasis of freshness and inspiration, if the oasis be no larger even than a table-cloth, than a desert of dreariness—larger than the Sahara. We can all be *in*tensive, even if we cannot yet be *ex*tensive; deep, if we cannot be wide; concentrated, if we cannot be diffused. The smallest pool of water can mirror the sun; it does not require an ocean. Let us live up to our possibilities for a single day, and we will not have to die to get to heaven ; we will be making heaven for ourselves and for others right here—to-day on this little spinning globe we call the earth.

What a man *is* at any moment of life does not fix what he may *become*. It is not necessarily a destination ; it may be merely a station ; a chapter, not the complete story. Progress is but the continuous revelation of possibilities transformed into realities. We see the running, but not the goal. It is not results that are the true test of living, for they may lie outside the individual's power to control, but it is ever the moral and mental qualities he puts into the struggle. The world's standard of judging is not in accord with the higher ethics of the soul. It is not getting the best, but proving worthy of the best, that is the revelation of true character.

The man who talks airily of the things he would do if only he had time, unconscious of the golden hours of wasted opportunity frittering idly through his fingers, had better wake up. He often envies those who have performed some marvel in self-education, when but a small section of the time he squanders in a year with the lavish recklessness of a Monte Cristo would enable him to learn a new language. Every hour is a new chariot of time's possibilities that might be laden with rich treasure, but if man tacks up the sign "no freight," he should not complain of the subsequent barrenness of result. The roll of the great leaders in human thought and effort have *not* been those who had the best opportunities, but those who made—the best use of them.

There are men battling with the soil on poor, anemic farms, that yield but a bare living, while underneath those acres may be rich veins of coal, wells of oil, that need but the revealing, or beds of other minerals that mean liberation from the slavery of poverty. It is not easy to make them manifest, but the greater treasures of the individual's possibilities within his own heart, mind and life he *can* bring out if he only will. Self-confidence is a virtue that should never lead a single life; it should be wedded—to tireless energy.

There come high-tide moments in all lives when contemplating some heroic deed, when our ears are filled with the triumphal music of a great thought, when the vitalizing words of some great thinker or teacher reach our soul through our eyes with a message of illumination. We then see our life in new perspective.   The meanness and emptiness of living on low levels shame the soul out of self-complacency, and we seem to see wondrous visions of our possibilities, glimpses of what we might become.   It is a coming face to face with our higher self that may re-create our lives for all the years if we only will. Let us realize our progressive possibilities, make them real, vital, growing, not uselessly held—as a warm living seed may rest for years in the dead hand of a mummy.   Realizing possibilities is the soul of optimism, and optimism is the soul of living.

III

Facing the Mistakes of Life

THERE are only two classes of people who never make mistakes,—they are the dead and the unborn. Mistakes are the inevitable accompaniment of the greatest gift given to man,—individual freedom of action. If he were only a pawn in the fingers of Omnipotence, with no self-moving power, man would never make a mistake, but his very immunity would degrade him to the ranks of the lower animals and the plants. An oyster never makes a mistake,—it has not the mind that would permit it to forsake an instinct.

Let us be glad of the dignity of our privilege to make mistakes, glad of the wisdom that enables us to recognize them, glad of the power that permits us to turn their light as a glowing illumination along the pathway of our future.

Mistakes are the growing pains of wisdom, the assessments we pay on our stock of experience, the raw material of error to be transformed into higher living. Without them there would be no individual growth, no progress, no conquest. Mistakes are the knots, the tangles, the broken threads, the dropped stitches in the web of our living. They are the misdeals in judgment, our unwise investments in morals, the profit and loss account of wisdom. They are the misleading by-paths from the straight road of truth—and truth in our highest living is but the accuracy of the soul.

Human fallibility, weakness, pettiness, folly and sin are all—mistakes. They are to be accepted as mortgages of error, to be redeemed by wiser living. They should never weakly be taken as justifying bankruptcy of effort. Even a great mistake is only an episode—never a whole life.

Life is simply time given to man to learn how to live. Mistakes are always part of learning. The real dignity of life consists in cultivating a fine attitude towards our own mistakes and those of others. It is the fine tolerance of a fine soul. Man becomes great, not through never making mistakes, but by profiting by those he does make; by being satisfied with a single rendition of a mistake, not encoring it into a continuous performance; by getting from it the honey of new, regenerating inspiration with no irritating sting of morbid regret; by building better to-day because of his poor yesterday; and by rising with renewed strength, finer purpose and freshened courage every time he falls.

In great chain factories, power machines are specially built to test chains—to make them fail, to show their weakness, to reveal the mistakes of workmanship. Let us thank God when a mistake shows us the weak link in the chain of our living. It is a new revelation of how to live. It means the rich red blood of a new inspiration.

If we have made an error, done a wrong, been unjust to another or to ourselves, or, like the Pharisee, passed by some opportunity for good, we should have the courage to face our mistake squarely, to call it boldly by its right name, to acknowledge it frankly and to put in no flimsy alibis of excuse to protect an anemic self-esteem.

If we have been selfish, unselfishness should atone; if we have wronged, we should right; if we have hurt, we should heal; if we have taken unjustly, we should restore; if we have been unfair, we should become just. Regret without regeneration is—an emotional goldbrick. Every possible reparation should be made. If confession of regret for the wrong and for our inability to set it right be the maximum of our power let us at least do that. A quick atonement sometimes almost effaces the memory. If foolish pride stands in our way we are aggravating the first mistake by a new one. Some people's mistakes are never born singly—they come in litters.

Those who waken to the realization of their wrong act, weeks, months or years later, sometimes feel it is better to let confession or reparation lapse, that it is too late to reopen a closed account; but men rarely feel deeply wounded if asked to accept payment on an old promissory note—outlawed for years.

Some people like to wander in the cemetery of their past errors, to reread the old epitaphs and to spend hours in mourning over the grave of a wrong. This new mistake does not antidote the old one. The remorse that paralyzes hope, corrodes purpose, and deadens energy is not moral health, it is—an indigestion of the soul that cannot assimilate an act. It is selfish, cowardly surrender to the dominance of the past. It is lost motion in morals; it does no good to the individual, to the injured, to others, or to the world. If the past be unworthy live it down; if it be worthy live up to it and—surpass it.

Omnipotence cannot change the past, so why should *we* try? Our duty is to compel that past to vitalize our future with new courage and purpose, making it a larger, greater future than would have been possible without the past that has so grieved us. If we can get real, fine, appetizing dividends from our mistakes they prove themselves not losses but—wise investments. They seem like old mining shares, laid aside in the lavender of memory of our optimism and now, by some sudden change in the market of speculation, proved to be of real value.

Realizing mistakes is good ; realizing *on* them is better. When a captain finds his vessel is out of the right channel, carried, by negligence, by adverse winds or by blundering through a fog, from the true course, he wastes no time in bemoaning his mistake but at the first sunburst takes new bearings, changes his course, steers bravely towards his harbour with renewed courage to make up the time he has lost. The mistake means —increased care and greater speed.

Musing over the dreams of youth, the golden hopes that have not blossomed into deeds, is a dangerous mental dissipation. In very small doses it may stimulate ; in large ones it weakens effort. It overemphasizes the past at the expense of the present; it adds weights, not wings, to purpose. "It might have been" is the lullaby of regret with which man often puts to sleep the mighty courage and confidence that should inspire him. We do not need narcotics in life so much as we need tonics. We may try sometimes, sadly and speculatively, to reconstruct our life from some date in the past when we might have taken a different course. We build on a dead "if." This is the most unwise brand of air-castle.

We go back in memory to some fork of the road in life and think what would have happened and how wondrously better it would have been had we taken the other turning of the road. "If we had learned some other business;" "If we had gone West in 1884;" "If we had married the other one;" "If we had bought telephone stock when it was at 35;" "If we had taken a different course in education;" "If we had only spent certain money in some other way,"—and so we run uselessly our empty train of thought over these slippery "ifs."

Even if these courses might have been wiser, and we do not really know, it is now as impossible to change back to them as for the human race to go back to the original bit of protoplasm from which science declares we are evolved. The past does not belong to us to change or to modify; it is only the golden present that is ours to make as we would wish. The present is raw material; the past is finished product,—finished forever for good or ill. No regret will ever enable us to relive it.

The other road always looks attractive. Distant sails are always white; far-off hills always green. It may perhaps have been the poorer road after all, could our imagination, through some magic, see with perfect vision the finality of its possibility. The other road might have meant wealth but less happiness; fame might have charmed our ears with the sweet music of praise, but the little hand of love that rests so trustingly in ours might have been denied us. Death itself might have come earlier to us or his touch stilled the beatings of a heart we hold dearer than our own. What the other road might have meant no eternity of conjecture could ever reveal; no omnipotence could enable us now to walk therein even if we wished.

We cannot relive our old mistakes, but we can make them the means of future immunity from the folly that caused them. If we were impatient yesterday, it should inspire us to be patient to-day. Yesterday's anger may be the seed of to-day's sweetness. To-day's kindness should be the form assumed by our regret at yesterday's cruelty. Our unfairness to one may open our eyes to the possibility of greater fairness to hundreds.

It is a greater mistake to err in purpose, in aim, in principle, than in our method of attaining them. The method may readily be modified; to change the purpose may upset the whole plan of our life. It is easier in mid-ocean to vary the course of the ship than to change the cargo.

Right principles are vital and primary. They bring the maximum of profit from mistakes, reduce the loss to a minimum. False pride perpetuates our mistakes, deters us from confessing them, debars us from repairing them and ceasing them.

Man's attitude towards his mistakes is various and peculiar; some do not see them; some will not see them; some see without changing; some see and deplore, but keep on; some make the same mistakes over and over again, in principle not in form; some blame others for their own mistakes; some condemn others for mistakes seemingly unconscious that they themselves are committing similar ones; some excuse their mistakes by saying that others do the same things, as though a disease were less dangerous when it becomes—epidemic in a community.

Failure does not necessarily imply a mistake. If we have held our standard high, bravely fought a good fight for the right, held our part courageously against heavy opposition and have finally seen the citadel of our great hope taken by superior force, by overwhelming conditions, or sapped and undermined by jealousy, envy or treachery we have met with failure, it is true, but—we have not made a mistake.

The world may condemn us for this non-success. What does the silly, babbling, unthinking world, that has not seen our heroic efforts, know about it? What does it matter what the world thinks, or says, if we know we have done our best? Sometimes men fail nobly because they have the courage to forego triumph at the cost of character, honour, truth and justice.

Let us never accept mistakes as final; let us organize victory out of the broken ranks of failure and, despite all odds, fight on calmly, courageously, unflinchingly, serenely confident that, in the end, right living and right doing—must triumph.

IV

When We Forget the Equity

LIFE simplifies wonderfully if we stand on a truer base of interpretation. We lose much of the real joy of living because of—our one-sided view. We accuse Nature of playing favourites. We imagine she is giving us all the hard benches, and to others, seemingly, reserved seats of preferred positions with an unnecessary supply of easy cushions. We may think Nature strews the path of one with roses while working overtime in collecting the thorns for us. It seems she sends us the great real sorrows and hands our neighbours across the street only an occasional bonbon trouble put up in a perfumed, beribboned box.

We forget we know only part of their trial or sorrow—never all. We forget while we know all our troubles, we do not recognize all the good we might enjoy if we would— the unnoted things dear in our lives that should greatly lessen our pain. We forget the equity.

30

In business the equity is the net value of a house or other property over all mortages or claims against it. There is an equity in your favour, on a bookkeeping account, if what is owed you is more than the amount that you owe.

Two men may have all their possessions in the separate ownership of two houses. The one who has a three thousand dollar house free from debt may envy the owner of the ten thousand house next door, unknowing it is covered by an eight thousand dollar mortgage leaving this man's equity at two thousand dollars. The owner of the small house is the richer of the two men. It is the equity that proves it. The philosophy of the equity illuminates many of life's greatest problems. It may soften the pain and sweeten our living by showing how equity intensifies our optimism. Recognition of the equity helps us to retain our crown of individuality.

Under the seeming injustice of life Nature is constantly seeking—equalizing, balance, justice. Nature keeps books with the individual. Her justice consists neither in the debit nor in the credit side of her ledger, but in the difference, the net, the balance, the equity. What seems to us injustice is often

really only our concentration on one side of
the account, to the exclusion of the other.
We exaggerate our sorrows so that they
eclipse our joys.   We are unjust to what we
have in hungering for what we have not; we
make our unsatisfied desires, not our possessions, the test of happiness.

Sometimes, with a sigh on our lips and a
sob creeping into our throat, we face our life
in numb rebellion.   We are so vividly conscious of what we have to bear that we may
forget our reason for happiness.   Our sorrows, seen through the magnifying glass of
discouragement, loom large before us.   Our
joys through the reducing glass of unsatisfied
desire minify into almost—nothingness.   We
permit what we lack to poison the waters of
what we have.   We forget the equity.   We
forget the big, clear, broad sweep of net happiness still remaining to us.   The mortgage
of care, sorrow, and responsibility blinds us
to our *real* possessions.

There are times when some affliction, some
illness holds us in its close deadly pressure.
The pain seems beyond the bearing.   It
seems so unjust, so cruelly hard to suffer.   It
mars our life; disturbs the simple sweetness
of the best in our nature; keeps us ever
slaves under the awful spell of its presence or

under the grim tyranny of fear of its recurrence. It makes us sometimes bitter and unjust in our poor misleading speech. But in our temporary times of relief the tide of courage, love, gentleness, tenderness runs just as strong as ever, just as earnest, in the high sea of our heart's desire.

If we can remember the equity we can make slightly easier this bed of pain. We may find joys in thought that lull the pang. We may find our place in life a little softened from the struggles of the past, some good fortune may add to our equity ; the touch of some inspiring friendship may hearten us to new bravery. We may realize that, because of our very illness, in the windings of time, the craft of some great joy has sailed to us, along the river of sorrow, and anchored in our heart.

We may envy the fame, fortune, or prosperity of another, unknowing the mortgages of care, responsibility, opposition, and worry that reduce the realness of what he has. We might be unwilling to pay a small percentage of the price it has cost him. His net happiness may be really less than ours.

A business man may pass through fearful times of stress and storm, trying hard to keep the flag of hope ever flying, watching care-

fully for rocks of financial discredit, delayed
payments and heroic effort—to bring his ship
of enterprise safe into harbour. The em-
ployees, leaving at the stroke of the bell, may
go home and drop all thought of business.
They look with envy, perhaps, at his easy
position, thinking and knowing nothing of
his constant courageous battle. They like
the property, forget his mortgages of worry
and responsibility and overlook the sympathy
and better work and loyalty they would give
if they realized—the equity.

They who have no children feel they are
the one thing lacking for happiness. Those
who have them may concentrate on the hard-
ship of so many to feed and care for and edu-
cate. One may put too much stress on the
loss, the other too much on the responsibility.
Both may forget the equity.

One great reason for much of our manufactured sorrow and misery is that we meas-
ure our lives by what we judge of others,
not by true estimate of our own. Life in its
highest sense is not a competition with others
but with ourselves. Have you ever sat in
the local train and felt you were making
good time? Suddenly the express whizzes
by, with a rush and a roar, in the same direction on a parallel track. As you watch this

train your own seems not only making no progress whatever but seems actually going rapidly back on the track, nearer to its starting point. When the express disappears you become conscious that your train has really been cutting distance all the time. Of course we realize it is only an illusion. In our daily life we make similar mistakes that vitalize our sorrows and put happiness into a moaning restless sleep, with wet eyes at dawn, because we forget—the equity.

If we have really much to bear, our attitude is making the bearing harder. It is making our power over conditions less, their power over us more. Let a fresh, clear, bracing breeze of optimism and new courage blow through the soul. Let us forget our sorrows in remembering our joys ; lessen our pain in realization that our imagination is increasing it, Let us remember the equity, the great possibilities, powers, and possessions for good to ourselves and the world—still left to us. If even *then* it seem little, throw in great handfuls of hope, purpose, confidence, determination, courage. Let us make it seem greater —until it really becomes greater.

We are inclined to regard all happiness, success, and sunshine as our due, which we have earned somehow by merely coming into the world and consenting to live here, while—trial, sorrow and pain seem an unjust invasion of our individual rights. The possession that would be the crowning joy of one might be the useless encumbrance or the last stroke of despair to another. We forget the equity in judging ourselves ; we forget it in judging others.

In our bookkeeping in business we do not let some one's debit of one hundred dollars wipe out his thousand-dollar credit; we realize that the man has an equity of nine hundred dollars remaining ; that he has this amount still to his credit. Why do we not let such justice apply to the acts of others?

The friend who has been kind and generous to us for years, who has stood bravely by us in hours of darkness, whose hand has steadied us through a crisis, who should have many golden spots in memory to his credit, —may prove weak, may offend us, may even desert us. In our hurt we may let the act of a moment neutralize the years of constancy, truth, and loyalty,—one debit cancel in an instant his long account of credits. We make it harder for him, harder for ourselves, by forgetting the equity, by overlooking the margin still remaining to his credit. A little patience, a little tolerance, a little generous

waiting and watching before pronouncing
final judgment, may do wonders in this
weary world.

For years some man in public life may
have struggled by consecration to purpose,
by loyalty to principle, by faithful adherence
to duty, and at last—reached a pinnacle of
fame. The world honours him; his life is
held up as a model, an inspiration to the
young, a source of pride to all. But that
man may do a wicked thing, and the world
is startled by the discovery. Society says,
"Now he is unmasked; now we know his
real character!" One evil act becomes typ-
ical of a whole life. One evil act submerges
all the good of years of faithful service.

Does society ever make one good act the
expression of a character? Does it ever let
one good act sweep like a mighty tide over a
wicked life and bury it forever from sight and
memory? That man's character may not
have been hidden. There may have been a
sudden temptation, one that came when mind
was weary, hope weak, and body worn, every
sentinel against sin, for the time, withdrawn—
and the victory was an easy one. Under the
compelling power of an act once committed,
morally dazed, he may have involved himself
further—doing what he could, not what he

should.   The act was wrong,   It was a big black mortgage on a life; but the equity, the justice of the balance of good, is his—and we wrong him by forgetting it.

Poets, preachers, teachers, delight to say character is a mighty structure, put together block by block, which may be ruined in an instant, fall into dust and chaos by one evil deed.   It is not so—this is cruelly unjust, untrue.   Character cannot be killed in an instant—it is only reputation that can be slain by one act.   Great single deeds do not make character—large single evil acts cannot ruin it.   Character is built of trifles.   The real test is the equity,—the balance of the good over the evil.

It may be the Infinite will finally so judge us; that He will regard no single black act as being our whole life; that He will judge us by our equity, letting good impulses, high motives, faithfulness in little things, true un-selfishness, brotherly love, kindness, and exalted ideals, balance, offset, and neutralize many of the acts of our human weakness, as we—in our poor human recognition of justice —permit a payment on account to cancel part of a debt.

V

The Crown of Individuality

THE supreme courage of life is the courage of the soul. It is living, day by day, sincerely, steadfastly, serenely,—despite all opinions, all obstacles, all opposition. It means the wine of inspiration for ourselves and others that comes from the crushed grapes of our sorrows. This courage makes the simplest life, great; it makes the greatest life—sublime. It means the royal dignity of fine individual living.

Every man reigns a king over the kingdom of—self. He wears the crown of individuality that no hands but his own can ever remove. He should not only reign, but—rule. His individuality is his true self, his best self, his highest self, his self victorious. His thoughts, his words, his acts, his feelings, his aims and his powers are his subjects. With gentle, firm strength he must command them or, they will finally take from his feeble fingers the reins of government and rule in his stead. Man must first be true to himself or he will be false to all the world.

Man reigns over this miniature kingdom of self—alone. He is as much an autocrat as is God in ruling the universe. No one can make him good or evil but he, himself. No one else in all the world has his work or his influence. Each of us can carry a balm of joy, and strength, and light, and love to some hearts that will respond to no other. Each can add the last bitter drop in the cup of life to some one dependent on us through love or friendship. No other in all the world can live our life, loyally fulfill our duties, or wear the crown of our individuality. It is a wondrous joy and inspiration to us if we see this in its true light, for never again would we ask: "What use am I in the world?"

When God "created man in His own image" His first gift to him was—dominion. The greatest dominion is over—self. Our lives should be vital to those around us. Each of us can be the sun of life in the sky of some one—perhaps many. Were we suddenly to have made luminant to us in every vivid detail our daily influence we should stand stunned by the revelation as was Moses in reverent expectancy before the burning bush.

The realization of the glory of the crown of our individuality would sweep the pettiness of selfish living and the wonder of the unanswerable eternal problems alike into— nothingness.

The world needs more individuality in its men and women. It needs them with the joy of individual freedom in their minds, the fresh blood of honest purpose in their hearts, and the courage of truth in their souls. It needs more people daring to think their own highest thoughts and strong vibrant voices to speak them, not human phonographs mechanically giving forth what some one else has talked into them. The world needs men and women led by the light of truth alone, and as powerless to suppress their highest convictions as Vesuvius to restrain its living fire.

They have the glad inspiring conscious- ness that they are not mere units on the census list, not weak victims of their own impulses, not human bricks baked into deadly uniformity by conventionality, but themselves —individuals. They are not faint carbon copies of others but strong, bold-print originals,—of themselves. They are ever lights not reflections, voices not echoes. To them the real things of life are the only great ones, the only objects worth a hard struggle.

In our darkest hours new strength always

comes to us, if we believe, as the silent stars shine out in the sky above us—when it is dark enough.   The hardest battle for our highest self is, when hungry for love and companionship of the soul, we must fight on —alone.   If we have one or two dear loyal ones watching bravely by our side, understanding us with a look, heartening us with a smile or inspiring us with a warm hand-pressure, we should fairly tingle with courage and confidence.

But if these leave us, slip away under the strain, or even betray us, let us face alone the seemingly empty life that is left us, just as heroically as we can.   Let us still stand in silent strength, like a lone sentry keeping guard over a sleeping regiment, in the grim shadows of night, forgetting for a time the terror of the solitude, the darkness, the loneliness, the isolation and the phantom invasion of memories that will not stay buried, in the courage that comes from facing an inevitable duty with a sturdy soul.   Of course it is not easy to live on the uplands of life.   It was never intended to be easy, but oh—it is worth while.

Individuality is the only real life.   It is breathing the ozone of mental, moral, spiritual freedom.   Nature made the countless thousands of flowers, trees, birds and animals without permitting two to be precisely alike. She stamped them with—individuality. She did it in a greater way for man. Some people seem to spend most of their time— trying to soak off the stamp. They follow in the footsteps of the crowd, guided by their advice. They wear a uniform of opinion ; suffer in the strait-jacket of silly convention, seek ever to keep in step with the line, and march in solid sameness along the comfortably paved road of other people's thinking,—not their own.

Individuality means stimulating all the flowers of our best nature and banishing one by one the weeds of our lower self. It means kingship over self and kinship with all humanity. It means self-knowledge, self-confidence, self-reliance, self-poise, self-control, self-conquest. It is the fullest expression of our highest self, as the most perfect rose most truly represents the bush from which it blossoms.

Individuality is the complete self-acting union and unity of man's whole mind, nature, heart and life. It is moved ever from within, not from without. The automobile is a type of individuality—it is neither pushed, pulled nor propelled by outside forces. The automobile is self-inspired, self-directed and self-moving.

Eccentricity is not individuality—it is a warped, unnatural distortion, like a reflection from a concave or convex mirror. Hypocrisy is not individuality—a mask is never a face and no matter how close it be held to the skin it never becomes a real face. Conventionality is not individuality—it is the molding of all that is vital and original in us to conform to an average type. Affectation is not individuality—it is only pretentious display of qualities one has not in stock. Individuality permeates every thought, word and act of ours as a half grain of aniline will tinge a hogshead of water so that the microscope will detect the colouring matter in every drop. Individuality crowns every expression of itself, in every day of living, with the—crown of its own kingship.

He who is swerved from a course he knows is right, through fear of ridicule, taunts, sneers or sarcasm of those around him, is not a man—self-directed by right. He is only a weak puppet pulled by the strings of manipulation in the hands of others. He is a figure in a moral Punch and Judy show—without its entertaining quality.

The man who knows he is doing wrong,

may realize it coolly, calmly, considerately, and even confess it with a sort of bravado, while he is too cowardly and selfish to do the imperative right is not—a king over his higher self but a weak slave of his lower self. That he knows the right and sees it without illusion merely emphasizes the depth of the abyss into which he has fallen.

The woman who lets bitterness grow in her heart until it poisons judgment, kills the love that was dear to her, deadens all her finer emotions and lets petrified prejudice usurp the throne of her justice while she shuts her ears to all pleas for understanding, commits one of those little tragedies in every-day life that may scar for years the soul of the one so cruelly misjudged. She may recklessly throw the golden crown of her individuality, with all its dear, sweet love and tenderness, into the weary loneliness of the years.

He who, from sheer lack of purpose, drifts through life, letting the golden years of his highest hopes glide empty back into the perspective of his past while he fills his ears with the lorelei song of procrastination is working overtime in accumulating remorse to darken his future. He is idly permitting the crown of his individuality to remain an irritating symbol of what *might be* rather than a joyous emblem of what *is*. This man is reigning, for reign he must, but he is not—ruling.

Individuality does not mean merely being our self, but our—highest self. It never means living for self alone. The world, in every phase, must be saved by—individuals. You cannot take humanity in mass up in moral elevators; they must receive and accept good as individuals. The united work of individuals makes up the action of society. It is easier to stimulate the individual to action than it is to galvanize society, as it is easier to lift one stone than a cathedral. As we intensify true individuality we at the same instant begin a fine coöperation with the best work of all humanity.

Individuality is the link; coöperation is the chain. You can strengthen the chain only as you strengthen the link. Christ, the great individualist, knew no shadow of selfishness. He sought to make better, stronger links in the living chain of humanity. His influence was ever an inspiration. He represented perfected individuality and individual perfection.

Let us reign a king over our individuality by conquering every element of weakness within us that keeps us from our best and raising every element of strength to its highest power by living in simple harmony with our ideals. We should begin it to-day. To-day is the only real day of life for us. To-day is the tomb of yesterday, the cradle of to-morrow. All our past ends in to-day. All our future begins in to-day.

Let us seek to reign nobly on the throne of our highest self for just a single day, filling every moment of every hour with our finest, unselfish best. Then there would come to us such a vision of the golden glory of the sunlit heights, such a glad, glowing tonic of the higher levels of life, that we could never dwell again in the darkened valley of ordinary living without feeling shut in, stifled, and hungry for the freer air and the broader outlook.

If at the close of day we can think of even *one* human being whose sky has been darkened by our selfishness, one whose burden has been new-weighted by our unkindness, one whose pillow will be wet with sobs for our injustice, one whose faith in humanity has been weakened at a crucial moment by our bitterness or cruelty, let us make quick atonement. Let us write the letter our heart impels us to write, while foolish pride would stay the hand; let us speak the confession that will glorify the lips we fear it may humiliate; let us stretch out the hand of love in the darkness till it touches and inspires the faithful one that possibly never caused us real pain.

Let us have that great pride in our individuality that would scorn to let petty pique or vanity keep us from doing what we know is right. Wear the robes of your royal pride in such kingly fashion that it would seem no sacrifice to stoop to brush off that which might stain them.

Let us make this life of ours a joy to ourselves and a tower of strength to others. Then shall we have made this life a success, no matter what its results. We shall have made character—and character is real life.

Let us live with our faces turned ever courageously to the East for the faintest sunrise of new inspiration. Let us realize that the four guardians of the crown of individuality are Right, Justice, Truth, and Love. Let us make Right our highest guide, Justice our finest aim, Truth our final revelation, and Love the constant atmosphere of our living. Then truly will we reign and—rule. It is not the extent of the kingdom but the fine quality of the kingship that really counts.

VI

Optimism that Really Counts

OPTIMISM is the sunshine of the soul radiated in action. It is true religion as a living, compelling fact—not a mere theory. It is sturdy confidence that right must triumph—united to tireless courage to make it triumph. Optimism is the finest weapon in the armoury of the individual. It unifies all the aggressive undaunted virtues of his strength into a force and an inspiration. It means fighting for, or with, the battalions of right, love, justice and truth—with determination to win. True optimism is something more than a continuous performance of hope. It is the joy of living—made an actual fact. It means seeking the best, living the best, doing the best. It means focusing all that is highest in our character to meet conditions.

Merely thinking, hoping and trusting that somehow, somewhere, somewhen, things will come out right while we do nothing to make them come out right is sunstruck folly—not optimism. It is a hammock philosophy for a sultry day when you are too drowsy to think and really do not care what whimsey of non-thinking plays games in your mind. No farmer outside of the pages of " The Arabian Nights " would expect nature alone to seed and fertilize and plow his fields and then to harvest his crops and put them in his barns without any human help whatever but his thinking. The exaggerated belief in the superhuman effect of thought as a direct power, is the folly of many.

This truly comfortable restfulness is merely a perfumed hot-air sentimentality. It dulls moral energy and deadens purpose. It is opiatism—not optimism. It is only mental or moral laziness wearing a rainbow robe of beautiful confidence. It may give a temporary fictitious strength to character but is ever revealed as weakness—in a crisis. It is only a papier-mâché shield—punctured in the first battle with the stern realities of life.

There is a light, jaunty, bubbling, care-free humour that takes the low fences of petty worries—neatly, gracefully. It smiles nonchalantly because it has never seen real trouble. This light-weight philosophy usually wilts at the first touch of real sorrow, grief and loss, like a straw hat meeting a sudden rain-storm. This is a sort of kindergarten optimism that sees only the sun—untouched

by clouds.   Real optimism knows the sun is
ever shining—despite the dark, heavy clouds
that may obscure it.   It knows that darkness
is ever the herald and messenger of dawn—
the new illumination and inspiration that must
come.   True optimism seeks to live in the
broad sunlight—when it can.   It seeks to rest
serene and confident of the outcome—when
all seems dark.

Verestchagin, the great Russian painter,
had a glass studio constructed at his home
near Paris.   It revolved on wheels, moved
by a windlass placed near his easel, and he
was thus enabled to paint all day with the
sunlight falling—in one direction on his mod-
els and drapery.   He who has cultivated optimism to be part of the real equipment of
character thus turns constantly to the light of
truth, love and kindness and to the growing brightness of the *real* things of our
living.

Cheerfulness has done much good; it has
been stimulating, kindly and helpful.   It
causes a cheery message.   It often prevents
sorrow, worry, deep grief from becoming con-
tagious.   This cheerfulness is sweet when
natural; brave, strong, and sturdy when assumed.   Cheerfulness is a sort of germicide
of the emotions; it deadens their power to

injure others and soothes the individual.
But cheerfulness at its very best and highest
is not—optimism.   It has never the full, free
completeness, finality, depth of optimism.

Cheerfulness may be a blossom of which
optimism is the plant.   Cheerfulness may be
refreshing rills of which optimism is the foun-
tain.   Cheerfulness may be a smile on the
face; optimism is the smile in the heart—
when one is fighting hardest.   Cheerfulness
may be the gentle, bubbling voice of a hope-
ful temperament or a sunny disposition; optimism is the clear convincing, individual tone
of the finest depths of our character.

Optimism seeks to discover the good points
in the acts of those around us, to let their little weaknesses and failings fade into nothingness in the shadow of our charity.   It seeks
to emphasize their best, to recognize it, to
appeal to it, to call it forth and to develop it.
A smile, a word of sympathy, a touch of human kindness, a hand-clasp of fellowship, an
unexpected bit of tenderness, courtesy or con-
sideration will accomplish wonders.   It is
syndicating sunlight and that is what real
optimism is.   It has a cheering magic health-
ful power that no amount of criticism or re-
proof could accomplish in changing others.
True optimism must begin in the—thought.

It must be real and living in word, act, and
atmosphere.   It cannot be put on as a veneer
from the outside; such a pretence is a grand-
stand play, not a private performance.

Optimism cannot foresee the suffering that
may come to us, but we can sturdily deter-
mine the effect we will let it have on us.
Sorrow assumes so many guises but we must
all "drink our cup."   The most bitter of all
cups of sorrow comes from the hand that
should never be the one to force it to our
lips, or it is some cup that gives agony to us
because we cannot save another from it.
There is the stirrup-cup of parting, when we
turn our horse's head away from the inn of
our hope—never to return.   The quassia cup
made bitter by that from which it is cut and
more bitter in memory.

The loving-cup, when moistened by un-
meaning lips and passed to us, may later
seem to carry a note of treachery we may not
understand aright—till too late.   There is the
cup of consolation that kindly hands gently
press to fevered lips.   There is that greatest
cup of a final supreme grief like that given
to the great Optimist of Calvary that "could
not pass."   These are but types of the cups
of life.   We should drink them—if drink we
must—as Socrates bravely drank his poisoned

hemlock, valiantly quitting a world unworthy his noble life with them.

The man of optimism should be kindest in criticizing others and never put the hand of harsh judgment on the unhealed wound of another's sorrow. Keenly, vividly, personally conscious of the trials, cares, sorrow, hunger, loneliness and suffering of life, he knows how often he failed and still fought on till at last he found his way—back to the sunlight. The optimist believes courageously that there is a reserve strength in man that brings sudden new inspiration to bear or to conquer, like the unexpected arrival of new food or troops in a siege.

The optimist, with new courage in his heart, new determination in his mind, and rebel tears secretly gleaming near his eyes, may rise superior to all unjust assaults. He may accept needless pain without cynicism, may meet betrayal without thought of revenge, may have to battle face to face with cruel disappointment without flinching and yet be victorious in a bettered self though vanquished in what was dearest—the hope and heaven of his living.

Optimism realizes that life is bigger than any single battle. The true soul has no final Waterloo; it has only its latest defeat, with its golden message of why it failed and how it may win in the next conflict. There may be in a very defeat an unnoted victory within our own life—a new revelation of latent power, and a glow and tingle of new courage. This may come to us while the bugle notes of triumph of the enemy still ring in our ears, their flaunting shouts of victory yet telling us of the prize we have lost and their smiles of conquest hardly faded from their eyes and lips. Seeming defeat may force us to retreat to higher grounds, where we may stand in stronger array, reintrenched, reinspired—to fight harder than ever.

With true optimism, we can face poverty without permitting it to harden us ; we can meet trial and sorrow and remain calm and unworried, stand bravely when we do not see the way to walk. We can let the glow of optimism so warm our soul that we remain simple, strong, sincere, and unruffled despite any environment. We thus may conquer adverse conditions by making them powerless to harm us—when we are unable to change them. Optimism is the armour of brave souls who fight conditions and never surrender to domination by the darker side of life that dares to daunt them.

The optimism that counts does not let the

individual—take whatever thoughts may
come.   It is a power that enables him to a
degree to select his own thoughts, to stimulate and encourage those that add to his
strength, that are wings to his purpose, that
thrill his energy with new consciousness of
power.   He gains control over those memories that take the smile from his face,
strength from his mind and joy from his
heart.   Optimism inspires a man to reduce
all depressing effects to a minimum, to raise
resistance to a maximum.

We never make conditions easier by telling ourselves how awful our troubles are;
by feeding our griefs for fear they may die a
natural death ; by intensifying every element
of pain.   The optimism that is worth any-
thing makes one person smile at troubles
that would put another out of the running
altogether.   It finds joy because it is trained
to see the tiniest glint of it as a miner's eyes
are quick to recognize the slightest speck of
gold in his pan.   Optimism sees roses in
life because it is looking for them ; receives
love because it is exhaling it.   It forgets its
sorrows in counting anew its blessing.   It
makes life truer, higher and finer for self by
making it sunnier for others.   This is—the
optimism that counts.

The Dark Valley of Prosperity

THE great test of individual character is not struggle but attainment; not failure but success; not adversity but prosperity. When Nature wants to put a man through the third degree, she places near him his laurel wreaths of victory; she megaphones to him the world's plaudits of success; she parades stacks of newspaper clippings and magazine articles with his portraits; she clinks his money-bags in his ears, and she tells him confidentially of the world-changing power of his influence. She smiles on him kindly and murmurs, "Poor fellow, is he able to stand it?" Then she sends him for his test through—the dark valley of prosperity.

Few pass through it immune; few acquire no perversion of mind, few escape fractures of ideals or new dents in character. But when *one*, through it all, remains just as good and simple and lovable as when he began the trip, remains kindly, strong, sympathetic, sincere, and unspoiled, Nature is glad indeed to admit she has found—a real man, a big man, a great man.

It is called the dark valley of prosperity because it, so often, dims the vision to the finer realities of life. In the early stages, in the dimness, they cannot see their old friends as they pass. There comes a peculiarity of the extensor muscles which prevents their extending the hand to some one no longer necessary to them. They acquire a form of memory impairment which prevents them remembering past favours and debts of gratitude due to those who stood by them in their hours of need. They do not notice their increasing chest expansion.

In the dark valley, their dearest hopes and their high ideals often slip away—into the silence. For them are substituted avarice and ambition, dressed in a livery of gold, and the individual may near-sightedly mistake them for higher good. In the shadows, conscience, the eye of the soul, may become so dulled that it cannot see the distinctions between genuine honour and a dishonour lawyers inform them is technically legal.

Sometimes they grope along the way, unconscious of the great price that they are paying. Suddenly they may realize, under a burst of temporary sunlight in the valley, that they have somehow, somewhere lost love, sympathy, trust, confidence, sweetness of nature or something else that has been—dearest in the world to them. It has dropped away like a locket from an unguarded chain, and they may—never find it again.

It is sheer cant that would throw wealth, fame, prosperity and success into a moral dust-heap as vanities of the world. We all want them. Those who take a high moral pose against them are either envious or are elbowing their way to get front Pharisee seats in the temple of virtue. These things are not evil in themselves. They are great powers for good but they are not—life's greatest. They are less than the real joys, like love, that no money can buy. Their wrong is when acquired by a sacrifice of truth, honour, justice or the real virtues of life, or when consecrated to the selfish side of living.

Poverty, struggle, failure and adversity are not in themselves passports to saintship—though they have given moral strength and sweetness to thousands. They have their own hard, bitter temptations to meet face to face. Theirs is far from an easy fight—the daily hand-to-hand battle with fate. But their temptations are usually direct, bold, clearly defined and their joys require so little. The tempting tests of prosperity come in subtle guise, gilded, perfumed and masked.

Poverty knows the word "stealing"; wealth may think it "financeering." Poverty knows "envy of another's possessions"; wealth may assume taking a manufacturing plant as "a good business deal." It may then even, by some strange sophistry, justify itself by declaring they will do better for the people. Poverty knows hunger for bread; wealth may hunger for the money of the bread-earners. Poverty usually sees evil in its aggressive, hardest phases. Prosperity may find it hidden and unsuspected like Cleopatra's asp in a bouquet of flowers.

A very slight drop of the acid of prosperity will begin the revelation of character of the man—be he not big enough to be simple. The slightest elevation in position, the least new good fortune, some temporary elation may reveal it. Have you ever noticed the man who has made a bit of a success in the city and returns for a week to his native village? He says he has come back to see the folks but it is really to have the folks see him. He enjoys the envy he excites in those who have not, like him—lived in the city. He wants to get sunburned in the warmth and fervour of their admiration. He stretches at length in his tilted chair, locks his thumbs behind the armholes of his waistcoat, and plays a flute solo of vanity on his breast-bone, using the buttons as stops manipulated by his fingers.

He occupies the centre of the stage every minute with his monologue. There is a touch of swagger in his walk, an irritating undertone of tolerance and patronage in his speech, and that loud voice we involuntarily use with the deaf. He is his own Boswell and his own Gabriel. It is, perhaps, only a harmless brand of vanity, but it shows he is getting near to the entrance of—the dark valley. When a big, simple man of *real* fame comes back, the story of *his* deeds leaks out incidentally; it is not exploded like a bomb.

The author of a successful book may have won his honours because he wrote with serious purpose. His message was supreme— fee for delivery, secondary. But he may be attacked by the vertigo of money-making and forget everything else. Inspired by his publisher, he may galvanize an old earlier book of his youth or rush through a hasty new one to have it in print before the wave of his sudden fame has died on the shores of forgetfulness. This new book may fail because he fell into the pitfall of commercialism in—the dark valley of prosperity.

Successful artists and illustrators, in many instances, do not follow up the first successes that won them fame. They slur over their work; they stand still or they degenerate. They accentuate the superficial in their style and care little for the strength that once was vital. They repeat the same characters, merely in slightly changed positions, like a cheap stock-company with a small cast and a meagre wardrobe,—playing in repertoire. These men often say if one ventures to speak that kindly word of protest we should always give to the needy: "Oh, what difference does it make—it pays all right." They should find some good Samaritan to drag them from the dark valley of prosperity and put them back again in the sunlight of struggle and the inspiration of adversity.

The business man who began in a small way and suddenly finds fortune emptying cornucopias of gold into his lap may find it hard to keep his feet and not to lose his head. The demon of greed may transform him— he wants more. He is like the farmer who desired only the land that adjoined his farm —each addition increased the field of desire; the more he had the more he wanted. Then may come a million owning a man, not the man a million. To accumulate more, he may defy laws, bribe legislatures and buy judges. Like a modern Joshua, he seeks to command—the sun of justice to stand still. His chloroformed conscience sleeps so soundly that an earthquake would not jostle it.

Wealth often makes men who started in bravely with high ideals, and normal moral health, become cold, heartless, selfish and uncharitable as they walk through the dark valley of prosperity. They often become arrogant and have a tendency to expect argument to close when they speak. They seem to have a corner on judgment as if their eye alone saw the sun of truth, their wisdom alone plumbed the depth of great questions. The abnormal pressure of business often forces them into pleasures of which they count not the cost nor the character. They are often too busy to take stock of the goods of their soul. The culture of the higher affections and sentiments is often killed.

Trifles affect them strangely, they grow irritated, impatient, irrational, at finding even a crumpled rose-leaf in the golden couch of their insomnia. They become more and more suspicious, and hardly know whom to trust. They fear every one is paving the way for some deal; stealthily seeking to gain their influence or to subtract something from the useless pile of their surplus wealth. They can have but few trusted, genuine friends of the mind, heart and soul.

Let us live gladly and glowingly in the sunlight of real simple love that means our great all. With faith in those few around us that girdles our whole world, realizing the sweetness of honest true friendships that so inspire; happy in the noble round of loyalty, consecrating to-day's duties to usher in a finer to-morrow, so living in the joy of our simple life of unselfish realness that we shall be glad the trials, tests and temptations of the dark valley have actually snubbed us as too unimportant to notice.

If called upon to the burdens of the greater responsibility let us bear them bravely at our best and let nothing rob us of simplicity, sweetness, strength, sympathy and all that is sterling. The greatest men and women are ever the simplest. There are thousands who bear their great burdens of fame, success, prosperity or wealth and who remain happy as of old and unspoiled by it all. They must truly be rare characters, of fine resources of thought, heart and soul who can safely pass through—the dark valley of prosperity.

www.ingramcontent.com/pod-product-compliance
Lightning Source LLC
Chambersburg PA
CBHW030813090426
42737CB00010B/1260